WORKBOOK FOR TRAINING ELDERS
AS COMMUNION CELEBRANTS

IN THE CUMBERLAND PRESBYTERIAN CHURCH

Jointly published by the Discipleship Ministry Team
And
Pastoral Development Ministry Team
Of the
Ministry Council
Of the
Cumberland Presbyterian Church

Funded, in part, by your contributions to Our United Outreach.

First printing 2015

ISBN-13: 978-0692238974

ISBN-10: 0692238972

Table of Contents

How to Use this Workbook

This workbook is designed to be used in two ways, by two different people: by the elder who will be serving as Communion Celebrant and the ordained minister assigned to train elders in serving as Communion Celebrants. The bulk of the workbook (the right-hand side of the book) is the general text for elders to read and follow. The sidebars (the left-hand side of the book) are notes and times for those training elders to use as a training design. Trainers can also use these sidebars to write their own notes that they may want to stress in their training.

A. Introduction

2 minutes.

1. Welcome the elder or elders to the training and introduce its purposes.

3 minutes.

2. Then, invite them to recall an experience of celebrating the Lord's Supper that was especially meaningful and why. Begin by sharing your own experience in order to provide an example.

A. Introduction

1. You are a leader of a particular Cumberland Presbyterian church and you have been called to serve Communion in the absence of an ordained minister. This responsibility is huge because as Cumberland Presbyterians the Lord's Supper is one of two sacraments that we recognize as a community. The other is baptism. We have also said that as a regular practice these two sacraments will be administered by an ordained minister in the Cumberland Presbyterian Church who has been set apart for this particular purpose. So your church has indeed bestowed an honor on you and God has called you to perform a meaningful sacrament.

The purposes of this training are:
- To identify the role of elders in serving as Communion Celebrants as reflected in the Constitution;
- To explore the meaning of the sacrament of the Lord's Supper;
- To experience a model for planning worship, which includes the Lord's Supper;
- To plan strategies for preparing for and serving the people through the Lord's Supper;
- To develop leadership skills through the practice of actually serving as a Communion Celebrant;
- To affirm the holy calling elders have from God.

2. Let's take some time to reflect on this sacrament and what makes it so special. Recall an experience in your life of celebrating the Lord's Supper that was especially meaningful to you. What made it so special? Reflect on the experience, paying close attention to what you felt, tasted, heard, saw, and maybe even smelled. Perhaps you smelled the bread being baked before church or tasted a special juice or wine made by a church member. You may remember hearing the words your pastor spoke or felt the excitement of taking Communion for the first time.

1

Whatever your story, it is one that is uniquely yours and won't be repeated in exactly the same way for the rest of your life. Jesus has asked us to come and join his feast, to partake of the elements and in doing so to remember his life and sacrifice every single time we do it. Because of the unique nature of every community, it is your privilege and responsibility to take seriously your role as Communion Celebrant.

B. The Biblical Basis

1. There are many references to the Lord's Supper in the Bible, but the three below give a feel for the different texts that are found in the New Testament. You can find other texts in *The Book of Common Worship*:

Matthew 26:26-30 (NRSV) *²⁶While they were eating, Jesus took a loaf of bread, and after blessing it he broke it, gave it to the disciples, and said, "Take, eat; this is my body." ²⁷ Then he took a cup, and after giving thanks he gave it to them, saying, "Drink from it, all of you; ²⁸ for this is my blood of the covenant, which is poured out for many for the forgiveness of sins. ²⁹ I tell you, I will never again drink of this fruit of the vine until that day when I drink it new with you in my Father's kingdom." ³⁰ When they had sung the hymn, they went out to the Mount of Olives.*

Here is the text from which the Words of Institution are taken. Matthew includes the blessing, the words we say, and even the singing of a hymn. One can see how the order of worship for the Lord's Supper came about.

1 Corinthians 10:16-17 (NRSV) *¹⁶The cup of blessing that we bless, is it not a sharing in the blood of Christ? The bread that we break, is it not a sharing in the body of Christ? ¹⁷ Because there is one bread, we who are many are one body, for we all partake of the one bread.*

B. The Biblical Basis

5 minutes.

1. Start with a reflection about the Lord's Supper based on the scripture texts provided.

5 minutes.

2. Then allow the persons to respond to the question: What in these words is so important that they have remained virtually the same down through the ages and across denominations?

Again, the language of our celebration of the Lord's Supper comes straight from scriptures like this one. Paul's words echo the words of Christ at the Passover meal.

1 Corinthians 11:23-26 (NRSV) *²³For I received from the Lord what I also handed on to you, that the Lord Jesus on the night when he was betrayed took a loaf of bread, ²⁴ and when he had given thanks, he broke it and said, "This is my body that is for you. Do this in remembrance of me." ²⁵ In the same way he took the cup also, after supper, saying, "This cup is the new covenant in my blood. Do this, as often as you drink it, in remembrance of me." ²⁶ For as often as you eat this bread and drink the cup, you proclaim the Lord's death until he comes.*

This scripture highlights the importance of the institution of the Lord's Supper to the early church with Paul echoing the words of Christ. Today, we celebrate this sacrament in remembrance of Jesus.

    2. Take time to reflect on these three scriptures, asking yourself: What in these words is so important that they have been spoken through the centuries and across denominations.

C. A Study on the Value of Communion

5 minutes.

1. Read the excerpt about the movie *Places in the Heart.*

10 minutes.

2. Then invite persons to discuss the questions that follow.

C. A Study on the Value of Communion

    1. The following is an excerpt from the book *Praying the Movies,* by Edward McNulty, a devotion book that uses various movies as its theme. This excerpt raises the importance and value of Communion as a time of renewal and healing even in the most damaged and broken circumstances.

In Robert Benton's Places in the Heart, *a disparate and desperate group of Texans slowly become a family as they struggle toward a goal during the hard days of the Depression. Edna is widowed suddenly when her sheriff husband is accidentally shot by a drunken black teenager. The boy is lynched by her neighbors, and she is left with nothing but their mortgaged farm to make a living for herself and her young son and daughter, Frank and Possum. She accepts the offer of help from a black handyman, Moze, and against the advice of the banker holding the mortgage, decides to raise a crop of cotton. The banker forces her to take in his blind, unwanted brother-in-law, Will, as a boarder. Hostile at first, Will slowly begins to fit into the family, especially after a destructive tornado blows through the farm. He realizes how precious the children, whom he had regarded as nuisances, really are. At the crucial harvest time, he does what he can to help out, as does Edna's sister, Margaret and her husband, Wayne. The latter are going through their own crisis, Margaret discovering that Wayne was having an affair with the wife of their best friend. She allows the repentant Wayne to stay with her but angrily tells him he is never to touch her again.*

At harvest time, Edna and all join together to become the first to finish gathering the crop and delivering it to the local cotton gin. As Moze had counseled Edna, there is a hefty bonus for being first; the cash prize is just enough for her to save the farm and have enough to start another round of planting. Through tremendous effort they succeed, and Moze even manages to guide her through the process of negotiating a favorable price with the unscrupulous owner of the cotton gin. But Moze pays a price, for the Klan beats him and runs him out of town. But he leaves with the blessings of Edna, who assures him that no one else could have taken such an unlikely piece of land and unskilled workers and completed the harvest on time.

The last scene in the film takes place in the little clapboard church of the village. The choir finishes a song, and the pastor reads from First Corinthians, chapter 13. We see the estranged Wayne and Margaret sitting together and yet not really together, until the truth of the Apostle Paul's words apparently affects her. The camera shows us a close-up of her hand reaching over and clasping his. A smile of relief appears on Wayne's face. Caught up in Paul's beautiful words, Margaret allows the miracle of forgiveness to melt the cold, hostile wall she had erected between them.

Then we hear the strains of the hymn "In the Garden." The choir sings the words, which form the background to the pastor's voice. He is repeating again the familiar Words of Institution, also from Paul, that begin the sacrament of the Lord's Supper. The trays of bread and wine are then brought to the congregation and each person takes them and passes the elements to a neighbor. Everyone is there, including the cruel town banker and the mill owner. Then we are brought up short—Moze is present! But he has left town, and even if he hadn't, he wouldn't dare come to a white church in 1930s Texas! The elements continue their passage around the congregation. The children receive them. Then Edna—she passes it to her husband! But he is dead! He passes it to the black teenager, also dead! The scene fades to black, with the hymn coming to its conclusion.

What is happening? We "see" in this scene that closes the film an even greater miracle than Margaret's forgiving Wayne—a miracle of faith.

2. Now after reading this story, ask yourself these questions:
- What does this mysterious scene say to us about the sacrament of the Lord's Supper?
- How would you reply to the statement that someone doesn't belong at the Lord's Table?
- Do any of us "deserve" to receive the sacrament?
- On what basis are we included?
- How is the sacrament a means of grace?

As the film shows, communion can bring community and can heal the brokenness that is present in all congregations at one point or another. From this film we can learn that the sacrament Jesus Christ gave to his disciples so long ago is still a very real and dynamic sacrament for every member

5

of our churches. We can never know what struggles and hurts one brings to the table for God to heal.

D. The Role of Elder as Communion Celebrant

D. The Role of Elder as Communion Celebrant

5 minutes.

1. Read the articles and describe what they say about the elder's role.

1. Let's take a look at what the "Constitution" (found at the back of *The Confession of Faith for the Cumberland Presbyterian Church*) says about the role of the elder who is serving as a Communion Celebrant.

4.6 *The session may designate two elders, either of whom, when authorized by the presbytery, may administer the sacrament of the Lord's Supper to the congregation.* (This applies only to the Cumberland Presbyterian Church.)

5.6 *The presbytery is charged with pastoral oversight and has the responsibility to:* ...
p. Take special oversight of churches which do not have the services of a minister, appointing a minister to moderate the session; and, if necessary, authorize an elder designated by the session to administer the Lord's Supper to the congregation, provided that the elder shall be instructed by the committee on the ministry in the meaning of the sacrament and how it should be administered; the elder shall serve under the authority of an ordained Cumberland Presbyterian minister selected by the presbytery, and each grant of authority shall be for one year. (The portion concerning elders serving Communion applies only to the Cumberland Presbyterian Church.)

We would like to say that all Cumberland Presbyterian churches are able to employ a full-time minister, but this is not always the case. It is the role of the presbytery to make sure that there is a moderator of the session and someone to administer the sacraments. Because the sacrament of the Lord's Supper usually comes around more often than baptisms, there have been problems with presbyteries fulfilling that role. For this reason, the General Assembly took action to allow elders to serve Communion in their own churches when authorized and trained by the presbytery.

E. The Meaning of the Sacrament of the Lord's Supper

E. The Meaning of the Sacrament of the Lord's Supper

20 minutes.

1. Explain that each elder is to work on his or her "The Meaning of the Lord's Supper Worksheet" for 15 minutes and then the group will discuss their responses to the articles for 5 minutes.

2. Allow *15 minutes* break

1.   It is important for you as a celebrant to understand the meaning of the Lord's Supper. For this reason, there is a worksheet on the next page raising questions and citing articles of the "Constitution" and the *Confession of Faith* that deal with the Lord's Supper. Spend time answering these questions and talk to pastors and other elders about them so you have a clear understanding of what we believe as Cumberland Presbyterians when it comes to this sacrament. Having this understanding will help you when you begin serving Communion on a regular basis and can help you communicate to your church members what they are doing through this act of faith.

The Meaning of the Lord's Supper Worksheet

I.   If you were asked to explain to your congregation on Sunday morning what the Lord's Supper is, what would you say?

II.   What do these statements from the *Confession of Faith* suggest is important to remember about the sacraments—baptism and communion? Write down in your own words the key ideas in the space provided below each article.

5.14 *Christian worship includes proclaiming the gospel of Jesus Christ, celebrating the sacraments, reading and hearing the scriptures, praying, singing, and committing life and resources to God. This common worship of the church validates and sustains such other worship as the church finds meaningful for celebrating the living presence of God."*

5.16 *Sacraments are signs and testimonies of God's covenant of grace. Circumcision and Passover are the sacraments of the Old Testament; baptism and the Lord's Supper are the sacraments of the New Testament. They are given by God and through his presence, word, and will are made effective.*

5.17 *Jesus Christ ordained the sacraments of baptism and the Lord's Supper for the church. They are administered by and through the church as part of her common worship, being entrusted to properly ordained ministers under the authority of a judicatory of the church.*

III.   What is the meaning of the Lord's Supper as reflected in these articles from the *Confession of Faith*? Write down in your own words the key ideas in the space provided below each article.

5.23 *The Lord's Supper was instituted by Jesus Christ on the night of his betrayal. It is a means by which the church remembers and shows forth Christ's passion and death on the cross. The sacrament is also a perpetual means given to the church to celebrate and experience the continuing presence of the risen Lord and her expectation of the Lord's return.*

5.24 *The elements used in this sacrament are bread and the fruit of the vine, which represent the body and blood of Christ. The elements themselves are never to be worshiped, for they are never anything other than bread and the fruit of the vine. However, because the sacrament represents the Savior's passion and death, it should not be received without due self-examination, reverence, humility, and grateful awareness of Christ's presence.*

5.25 *This sacrament is a means of spiritual nourishment and growth, an act of grateful obedience to Christ, and a commitment to the work and service of Christ's church for all who celebrate it.*

5.26 *All persons who are part of the covenant community and are committed to the Christian life are invited and encouraged to receive this sacrament.*

5.27 *Each congregation should celebrate this sacrament regularly. Every Christian should receive it frequently.*

F. Planning for Worship and Celebrating the Lord's Supper.

3 minutes.

1. Remind the elders of Article 5.14 of the *Confession of Faith*. Ask them to read at home the "Directory of Worship" and call attention to the sections dealing with worship and worship leadership.

2 minutes.

2. Introduce the next steps in exploring the various elements in worship and then planning a worship experience that will include them serving as Communion Celebrants.

F. Planning for Worship and Celebrating the Lord's Supper

1. Read these words again from the *Confession of Faith*:

5.14 *Christian worship includes proclaiming the gospel of Jesus Christ, celebrating the sacraments, reading and hearing the scriptures, praying, singing, and committing life and resources to God. This common worship of the church validates and sustains such other worship as the church finds meaningful for celebrating the living presence of God.*

The Lord's Supper is celebrated in the context of worship, not as something isolated and apart from the community of faith. As such, your role in administering the sacrament applies to the context of worship. If worship is planned and led by some other person (e.g., a stated supply or unordained minister), then that person may plan the worship experience and you as elder will be responsible only for the administering of the Lord's Supper. However, if you alone are responsible, you must plan for Communion in the context of a worship experience for the congregation. Even if you are called upon to serve the sacrament to a homebound member, the administration of the sacrament is connected to the community of faith at worship the day the sacrament is celebrated. Taking it to other members is always in the context and an extension of the congregation's worship.

Refer to the "Directory of Worship," in the *Confession of Faith* and look at the sections dealing with worship and worship leadership. Study the entire directory before you begin administering the Lord's Supper.

2. The next steps toward serving as Communion Celebrant is to actually explore the various elements of worship and then plan a worship experience that will include your serving as Communion Celebrant.

Read section D from the "Directory of Worship" entitled "Suggested Orders for Corporate Worship." It may help you to go through and highlight each element, underlining a key sentence or phrase that describes each section. Pay special attention to each description even though you may have been worshiping all of your life.

As you read about each element, ask yourself this question: How can each element support your celebration of the Lord's Supper?

Each element of worship should connect with the theme of the scripture that is being proclaimed and can easily be highlighted within the Communion service. In this way, all elements of the worship service will reinforce the scripture used for that particular Sunday and will stress God's word for the hearers and worshipers.

5 minutes.

3. Ask elders to start reading section D and highlight each element and underline the key sentence or phrase that describes each section.

D. SUGGESTED ORDERS FOR CORPORATE WORSHIP

While there is no one order for worship which is appropriate for all Christians, there is a classic shape to corporate worship which informs all our worship. That shape is one of God's action and our response to God. The following orders for Christian worship are informed by that classical shape. The first order includes the celebration of the Lord's Supper, since the Lord's Supper is an act which gives the peculiar shape to all Christian worship.

1. Corporate Worship Including the Lord's Supper

Prelude
The corporate worship begins as Christians present themselves to join together to worship God. The music chosen for a prelude should enable people to focus their attention on God and God's kingdom. Worshipers are to be instructed that the prelude is a part of their corporate worship. It is not a "mood setter" or a time to "get ready" for worship. Perhaps ringing a bell before the prelude begins, or some signal from the leader of worship prior to the prelude indicating that worship is now to begin would be helpful. The liturgist may simply say, "Let us worship God." Then the prelude can begin.

Opening Sentences
Traditionally these sentences have always been scripture with the focus being on God and our relationship to him. The classic model for Presbyterian worship has been Psalm 124:8, "Our help is in the name of the Lord who made heaven and earth." Many other passages of scripture can be used as opening sentences, and may be said responsively. But whatever passages are used, they will emphasize why the participants have gathered and what they are about. The use here of any material other than scripture should be carefully examined as to substance and intent.

Hymn of Praise
The dominant purpose of Christian worship is praise—the joyful response of the people to God's unspeakable gift in Jesus Christ. It is highly appropriate, therefore, that the people sing their praise to God following the opening sentences. The hymn should be one whose tune and text point to God's greatness, majesty, love and goodness.

Prayer of Adoration
Ordinarily the prayer following the hymn of praise continues the theme of praise and adoration. Care should be taken to shape the prayer as one of adoration, and remember that other prayers in the service will be shaped by other appropriate prayer emphases.

Confession of Sin and Declaration of Pardon or Words of Assurance

The confession of sin and the assurance of forgiveness are an integral part of worship, just as they are an integral part of the Christian life. Historically this act is found in one of two places: following the act of adoration or before the celebration of the Lord's Supper.

It is in order to call the worshipers to confession through the use of scripture passages. The prayer of confession follows and often it is most meaningful when prayed in unison. If it is prayed by one person on behalf of all, it should be carefully planned and thoughtfully prayed so that it can indeed be a corporate prayer in which all may participate.

The act of confession is to be followed by a strong affirmation or declaration of pardon. Here again scripture provides the best treasury for such affirmation, and needs no comment of any kind. For example, I John 1:9 is often used: "If we confess our sins, God is faithful and just, and will forgive our sins and cleanse us from all unrighteousness."

Responses of Praise

A response of praise appropriately follows the act of confession and the granted forgiveness from God. This response can take several forms. Psalms and canticles (songs from the Bible other than those contained in the Psalter) have long been used for this purpose. The reading from the Psalter is appropriately followed by the singing of the Gloria Patri ("Glory Be to the Father"), or some other response of praise.

The Hearing of God's Word

The reading, proclaiming and hearing of God's word constitute the second major movement in the order of worship. We gather to hear God's word addressed to us through the reading of scripture and the preaching of the sermon. Here proclamation is central and uppermost.

The reading of scripture is of critical importance to proclamation. Whoever is responsible for reading it should be adequately prepared and possess the ability to read well.

In selecting the scripture passage or passages to be read careful thought is to be given to providing the worshipers with all the many and varied themes and emphases of God's word.

The use of a lectionary for corporate worship is highly recommended. A lectionary is a systematic ordering of scripture to ensure that the many themes of scripture will be read and provide the basis for proclamation. Traditionally lectionaries are developed around the Christian year and prescribe specific readings for each Sunday. It is also appropriate for those who design worship to produce a lectionary for use.

Customarily the reading of scripture is preceded by a *Prayer for Illumination* which calls upon God to enable us to be receptive to his word.

It is appropriate that the scripture readings be separated by an *anthem* or *canticle* or *hymn*.

The *sermon* appropriately follows the last scripture reading and ordinarily is to be based upon one or more of the readings. Care should be exercised that the sermon not violate the integrity of worship nor compromise the biblical witness. A prayer or *Ascription of Praise* appropriately follows the sermon.

Affirmation of Faith or Creed

The affirmation of faith by the worshipers has from the early years of the Christian movement been a central part of corporate worship. Historically the recital of the Creed or personal *Affirmation of Faith* was the basis on which worshipers were admitted to the Lord's Supper. Only those persons who were willing to say, "I believe…" were allowed to participate in the worship of the people of God at the table. Also, the *Creed* or *Affirmation of Faith* functions as a response to our hearing of God's word.

It is fitting also that an appropriate hymn be sung to express further the worshipers' belief or faith.

The Prayers of the People

The people's *Affirmation of Faith* is appropriately followed by the *Prayers of the People.* These are prayers that may be offered by a minister or a layperson to which all present can respond by saying, "Amen."

The *Prayers of the People* may include thanksgiving, supplication, intercession, and conclude with the Lord's Prayer. Thanksgiving lifts up the expression of gratitude common to all those present and may include appreciation for the church; supplication focuses on the needs of the worshipers both individual and corporate; intercession incorporates the needs of those not present but whose needs are well known, especially the needs of those who are not members of the Christian community; the Lord's Prayer is the model of all our prayers and enables all present to pray according to Jesus' teaching and understanding of prayer.

The Presenting of the Gifts or Offering

Historically the offering was the occasion in corporate worship when the elements of bread and wine which were to be used in the Lord's Supper were presented. It is appropriate to bring them to the communion table still, or if the table has already had the elements placed upon it, they are at this time prepared for the Lord's Supper which is to follow.

At this point in the service, money and other offerings are brought forward. The giving of money is to be seen as an act of worship, a symbol of our commitment as individuals and as a corporate body to the redemptive work of God in the world. Even if there is no money to be given as a part of a particular service of corporate worship, some act of self-giving is in order for that service. The Doxology may be sung as an act of praise following the giving of our gifts, and the act of giving may conclude with a *Prayer of Dedication.*

The Celebration of the Lord's Supper

The celebration of the Lord's Supper is central to Christian worship. In this liturgical act a visible presentation of the word is joined to it and proclamation. Together, sermon and sacrament bear witness to God's redemptive actions in the death and resurrection of Christ. It is always appropriate to include the sacrament as a part of corporate worship.

In celebrating the Lord's Supper, those designing worship should be guided by the acts which have traditionally accompanied that necessary part of corporate worship. Those acts may be identified by different names and be clustered under different headings, but essentially they are these:

a. *Invitation to the Lord's Table.* The minister who is to lead the congregation in celebrating the Lord's Supper invites all who believe in Jesus Christ as their Lord and Savior to participate in this celebration.

b. *Words of Institution.* Scripture passages which establish the warrant for this celebration are read or recited by the one who is designated to officiate at the communion table. Appropriate words are found in I Corinthians 11:23-26; Matthew 26:26-30; Mark 14:19-26, and Luke 22:19-20. Other passages of scripture which relate Jesus' meeting with his disciples for a meal after the resurrection may also be used for this purpose.

c. *Prayer of Thanksgiving.* This prayer most often includes an expression of thanksgiving to God for who he is and what he has done in Jesus Christ, a calling upon God to send the Holy Spirit upon the elements and the people, and an offering of the lives of the people to be used by God.

d. *Breaking and Pouring.* Action at this point in the liturgy is most meaningful. The acts of breaking the bread and pouring the wine dramatically remind us that Christ's body was broken and his blood was shed for all. It is important therefore that such action be thoughtfully done and clearly visible to all present. A loaf of bread of sufficient size needs to be provided for the breaking, and a chalice and flagon are necessary for the pouring. After the pouring, the chalice can be elevated for all to see. If the act of pouring is omitted, the chalice may still be elevated.

e. *Partaking of the Elements.* Different ways of distributing the elements have developed in the life and worship of the church which are appropriate. Congregations of the Cumberland Presbyterian Church/Cumberland Presbyterian Church in America have traditionally followed the procedure of serving the worshipers in their pews. Using this method, the minister may partake of the elements, then serve the ruling elders, who in turn serve the congregation; or the minister and ruling elders may serve others first and then serve one another.

Another method used is having the members of the congregation come forward to partake and be served by the minister and ruling elders. Still another approach is to have the worshipers come forward and be served while seated at a table.

In each method used, worshipers may stand, sit or kneel.

Many worshipers have found the use of one loaf of bread and one cup (traditionally called the "common cup") for all worshipers to be most meaningful. Some congregations use the common cup only for the minister and the ruling elders.

    f. *Post Communion Prayer.* A prayer of praise, commitment and intercession may follow the distributing of the elements. A canticle of the church or a hymn may appropriately follow this prayer.

    g. *The Dismissal/Charge/Benediction.* Corporate worship may conclude with a dismissal signaling the concluding of worship, or a charge in which the people are exhorted to go into the world to be the people of God, or a pronouncement of a blessing upon the people, or any combination of the three. Leaders are encouraged to use biblical material for this act.

Postlude

Like the prelude this music should be chosen with corporate worship in mind. Moreover, if it is to be a part of worship, then all present should be requested to remain silent and listen to the postlude and make it a part of their worship. If this is to happen, it means that in most instances the postlude will be brief. If the postlude is not to be understood as a part of worship, then it is recommended that it be removed from the order of worship and that the service conclude with the dismissal or benediction.

Announcements

Persons responsible for designing corporate worship will need to think through how the making of necessary announcements will relate to corporate worship. Some congregations will choose to present all necessary announcements in a bulletin and expect the worshipers to read them without any mention of them being made as a part of worship. Other congregations may decide to make announcements *prior* to the beginning of corporate worship. Another option is to make announcements after corporate worship.

Those congregations which decide it is the wise choice to make announcements as a part of worship should give thought to how this can be done without disrupting worship. One possibility is to make announcements just prior to the *Prayers of the People*, and incorporate the concerns of the announcements into the prayers. Whenever announcements are made as a part of corporate worship, they should be restricted to announcements that relate directly to the on-going mission of the congregation and have relevance for all members of the worshiping community.

2 minutes

4. Introduce the three worksheets: "Planning for Worship," "Resources for Worship," and "Prayers."

5 minutes

5. Tell them about the preparatory decisions that must be made before the worship experience can be planned.

4. On the next few pages are three worksheets: "Planning for Worship," "Resources for Worship," and "Prayers." These worksheets will help you complete your plans for your worship. However, before you begin, there are still a few decisions about celebrating the Lord's Supper that you need to make that will help you better prepare for the worship experience.

5. **Preparation for the Sacrament**—Make a list of the preparations that need to be made for the sacrament of Communion. Be sure the following are included:
- elements purchased/made and provided
- Communion ware ready
- mode of serving determined and elders assisting given instructions
- scriptures and prayers are identified

Methods and Modes of Serving. What ways of serving the Lord's Supper have you personally experienced? What is the typical method of serving and receiving the sacrament in your congregation?

There are 2 main methods of administering the sacrament:
- Persons come to the table to receive the elements
- Persons are served in their seats or pews and then serve one another

There are at least 3 ways of distributing the elements:
Intinction—Persons are invited to take a piece of bread from a loaf and dip it into a common chalice and then eat it
Common Cup—Persons receive and eat a piece of bread or a wafer and then drink from a common cup
Trays and Cups—Persons receive and eat the bread or wafer and then drink from a small, individual cup

You will need to determine the method and mode you will use and instruct the elders who are to help serve. If persons are coming to the front to receive Communion, you will also need to give special instructions about which aisles they will come and go in and which sections of the sanctuary will come first, etc. If you would like for people to come as they feel led, you may also specify that.

After you have made these decisions, begin spending some time with the three worksheets that will help you in your preparation for serving Communion.

18 minutes

6. Ask the persons to work on the "Planning for Worship Worksheet," with the help of the "Resources for Worship," and "Prayers" handouts. Invite them to complete the plans on the worksheet. Inform them that they will have an opportunity to use the plan as they practice leading worship and serving as Communion Celebrants later.

PLANNING WORSHIP WITH COMMUNION WORKSHEET

Prelude   selected

Opening Sentence(s)—Call to Worship

Prayer of Adoration/Opening Prayer

Hymn of Praise (title and number)

Confession of Sin (Select from Resources or use your own prayer.)

Declaration of Pardon or Words of Assurance (scripture)

Responses of Praise—Hymn (title and number)

Hearing of God's Word (Select scripture reading/include brief reflection, if desired.)

Prayers of the People (own prayer)

Presenting of Gifts/Offering (scriptural invitation)

Doxology or Dedicatory Prayer

Celebration of the Lord's Supper

1. Invitation to the Lord's Table (Select scripture.)

2. Words of Institution (Select scripture.)

3. Prayer of Thanksgiving (Use your own or one from "Worship Resources.")

4. Breaking and Pouring (Select words, action, how to do.)

5. Partaking of the Elements (how distributed/served)

6. The Prayer after Communion (Use your own or one from "Worship Resources.")

Hymn (title and number)

Charge (See "Worship Resources.")

Benediction/Blessing (See "Worship Resources.")

Postlude   selected

RESOURCES FOR WORSHIP

Call to Worship/Opening Sentences

Psalm 118:24	Psalm 106:1	Revelation 1:4-5	Psalm 34:3
Psalm 57:8-11	Psalm 95:1-2	Isaiah 40:31	Psalm 100:1, 2, 4
1 Peter 1:3	Isaiah 57:15	Psalm 46:1-3	John 4:24
Romans 12:1			

Call to Confession

Jeremiah 31:33-34	Hebrews 10:22	1 John 1:8-9	1 John 2:1-2
Hebrews 10:22	Isaiah 30:18	Hebrews 4:14, 16	Matthew 11:28-30
Romans 5:8	Hebrews 4:16		

Declaration of Forgiveness

Colossians 2:12	1 Timothy 1:15	Romans 8:34	Psalm 103:8, 10-12
Psalm 145:8-9, 18-19	2 Corinthians 5:17	1 Peter 2:24	Romans 6:8-11
2 Corinthians 5:17	Colossians 3:1		

Affirmations of Faith

The Apostle's Creed	Romans 8:35:37-39	Romans 8:1, 28, 38-39	Colossians 1:15-20
1 Corinthians 15:1-4	Mark 16:9	Matthew 16:16	Revelation 22:13
John 20:38	Philippians 2:5-11		

Offertory Scriptures

Ephesians 5:2	Matthew 6:19-21	Romans 12:6-8	2 Corinthians 9:6
Hebrews 13:16	Deuteronomy 15:11b	Deuteronomy 16:17	Psalm 116:12, 14
Acts 20:35b	1 Corinthians 4:2	1 Corinthians 9:10, 11	Psalm 24:1
Matthew 10:8b	2 Corinthians 8:9	2 Corinthians 9:7	Revelation 4:11
Psalm 50:14	Psalm 96:8	Matthew 5:23, 24	Romans 12:1
1 John 3:17, 18			

Invitations to the Lord's Table

Luke 13:29	Luke 24:30, 31	Matthew 11:28, 29	John 6:35, 37
Matthew 5:6	Revelation 3:20	Psalm 34:8	

Words of Institution:

Mark 14:19-26	Matthew 26:26-30	Luke 22:19-20	1 Corinthians 11:23-26

Charge and Blessing

Charge:

1 Corinthians 16:13	2 Timothy 2:1	Ephesians 6:10	1 Thessalonians 5:13-22
1 Peter 2:17	Luke 2:29-32	Colossians 3:17	Micah 6:8
1 John 3:23	Matthew 22:37-40		

Blessings:

2 Corinthians 13:14	Numbers 6: 24-26	Philippians 4:7	1 Thessalonians 5:23
Romans 15:13	Hebrews 13:20, 21		

ADDITIONAL HELPFUL RESOURCES: (Cumberland Presbyterian Resources at 901.276.4572 x252)
- *The Service for the Lord's Day: Supplemental Liturgical Resource 1.* Westminster Press, 1984. A collection of worship aids with prayers and scripture readings.
- *The Confession of Faith for Cumberland Presbyterians.* Office of the General Assembly, 1984 Revision.
- *The Book of Common Worship.* John Knox/Westminster Press. Includes worship services and liturgies for various occasions.

PRAYERS

Opening Prayers:
1. God of all glory, on this first day you began creation, bringing light out of darkness. On this first day you began your creation, raising Jesus Christ out of the darkness of death. On this Lord's Day grant that we, the people you create by water and the Spirit, may be joined with all your works in praising you for your great glory. Through Jesus Christ, in union with the Holy Spirit, we praise you now and forever. Amen.

2. O God, you are infinite, eternal, and unchangeable; glorious in holiness; full of love and compassion; abundant in grace and truth. All your works praise you in all places of your dominion, and your glory is revealed in Jesus Christ our Savior. Therefore, we praise you, blessed and holy Trinity, one God, forever and ever. Amen.

3. O God, source of all beauty and goodness, your grace comes fresh every morning. In each new day you give us light. We praise you for your never-failing love that satisfies our needs and shows us the way to follow. We rejoice in your constant care, for you are faithful in love for all people, offering your salvation through Jesus Christ. Amen.

Confessions of Sin:
1. Merciful God, we confess that we have sinned against you in thought, word, and deed. We have not loved you with our whole heart and mind and strength; we have not loved our neighbors as ourselves. In your mercy forgive what we have been, help us amend what we are, and direct what we shall be, so that we may delight in your will and walk in your ways, to the glory of your holy name. Amen.

2. Eternal God, in whom we live and move and have our being, your face is hidden from us by our sins, and we forget your mercy in the blindness of our hearts. Cleanse us from all our offenses, and deliver us from proud thoughts and vain desires. With lowliness and meekness may we draw near to you, confessing our faults, confiding in your grace, and finding in your our refuge and strength; through Jesus Christ your Son. Amen.

3. Almighty God, in Jesus Christ you called us to be a servant people, but we do not do what you command. We are often silent when we should speak, and useless when we could be useful. Have mercy on us, O God. Forgive us and free us from sin; through Jesus Christ our Lord. Amen.

Great Prayer of Thanksgiving:

Almighty God, creator and sustainer of life, your majesty and power, your continued blessings, and your great goodness fill us with wonder. We are unworthy of the pardon you have in mercy given. We can bring only our thanks, putting our trust in your Son, who alone saves us from evil. Therefore, in joy, with prophets, apostles, martyrs, and saints of every time and place, we join in giving you praise.

Holy, holy, holy Lord, God of power and might, heaven and earth are full of your glory. Hosanna in the highest. Blessed is he who comes in the name of the Lord. Hosanna in the highest.

God of glory, in thanks we remember how Jesus broke bread and gave the cup so that he might live in us and we in him.

God of mercy, in thanks we remember how Jesus invites us to his table, imprinting on our hearts his sacrifice on the cross. In gratitude we bow before the Righteous One, declaring his resurrection and glory, and knowing that his prayers alone make us worthy to partake of his spiritual meal.

Believing Christ's promise of eternal life, we live in him and declare: Christ has died, Christ is risen, Christ will come again.

Almighty God, pour out your Holy Spirit upon us, that as we receive bread and wine we may be assured that Christ's promise in these signs will be fulfilled.

Eternal God, lift our hearts and minds on high where, with Christ your only Son, and with the Holy Spirit, all glory is yours, now and forevermore. Amen. (Or you may lead into The Lord's Prayer.)

Prayers after Communion:

Gracious God, you have made us one with all your people in heaven and on earth. You have fed us with the bread of life, and renewed us for your service. We give ourselves to you, and ask that our daily living may be part of the life of your kingdom. May our love be your love reaching out into the life of the world; through Jesus Christ our Lord. Amen.

G. Serving as Communion Celebrant.

40 minutes.

Have available bread and juice and communion ware—chalice and paten, communion tray with glasses, etc. Go into a sanctuary if one is available. Invite the elder or elders to help set up the communion table and prepare the elements. (They may actually get someone else to do this in their congregations, but for the practice, invite them to do it during this training.) Invite elders to determine the mode they will use and the assistance needed.

Gather close to the communion table. Have the elder or elders bring the completed "Planning for Worship" worksheet with them. If more than one elder is being trained, go through the "Order of Worship" with each elder contributing a particular element of the worship. For example, elder A may read his or her "Call to Worship," elder B might offer the opening prayer, elder C might do the scripture, etc. When you reach the celebration of the sacrament, demonstrate first the breaking and lifting of bread and the pouring and lifting of the cup

G. Serving as Communion Celebrant

Now that you have learned about the Lord's Supper and have planned your worship service including Communion, it will be helpful to go through the motions of serving Communion. With a pastor mentor, set aside a time and serve Communion to him or her using all of the words and actions that you will in a regular worship service. Have bread and juice and Communion ware, which includes either a chalice and paten or plate and Communion tray with glasses. Use your sanctuary, if it is available. You may actually have someone who regularly prepares the elements for Communion in your congregation, but for the practice and to orient yourself to all of the senses, do this preparation yourself this first time. You may want to have several elders with you to serve the elements as it will be done in regular church services.

Invite your pastor mentor to demonstrate first the breaking and lifting of bread and the pouring and lifting of the cup before you do it. This may take some time, but it is necessary "practice" to learn how to serve as Communion Celebrant, so it is something to take seriously.

Above all, relax and enjoy this experience. Most ministers can tell you stories about mishaps and humorous things that have happened to them while serving Communion. Know that things are bound to happen and few if any people have ever left the church because the Lord's Supper was not served

TRAINER'S NOTES

before elders are invited to do so. This will take some time, depending on the number of elders, but it is necessary practice to learn how to serve as a Communion Celebrant.

5 minutes.

Questions. Following the practice of serving communion, respond to questions from the elder or elders. Make sure that their questions are answered. If you cannot do it, help them to find the answer.

5 minutes.

Closing. Gather in a circle, join hands, and pray a prayer of thanksgiving to God for having *called* this elder or these elders through their church sessions to serve as Communion Celebrants. Invite God's blessings on them as they go forth to fulfill the purpose for which they have been called. Pray for wisdom and courage as they plan and provide leadership for worship in which the Lord's Supper is celebrated.

If you wish, provide a certificate of training for each elder that indicates the date on which he or she completed preparation to serve as a Communion Celebrant.

perfectly. But also remember that this time is one when God is working through you and it is God's table and not yours. God will do what God will do, so feel the Holy Spirit's leading.

It would be most appropriate to ask your presbytery to bless you in this ministry. You may want them to pray a prayer of thanksgiving to God for having called you through your church session to serve as a Communion Celebrant. Their prayer may also invite God's blessings on you as you go forth to fulfill the purpose for which you have been called and pray for wisdom and courage as you plan and provide leadership for worship in which the Lord's Supper is celebrated. Presbyteries may also provide a certificate of training, indicating the date on which you completed preparation to serve as a Communion Celebrant.